Anna O'Kelly

Bealaí Ealaíonta

Bealaí Ealaíonta
(Artful Paths)

Text by
Anna O'Kelly
as told to
Kristi Collins

Photographs by
Úna Ní Shé

Design by
Kristi Collins and Úna Ní Shé

Layout by
Kristi Collins

Artwork by
Anna O'Kelly

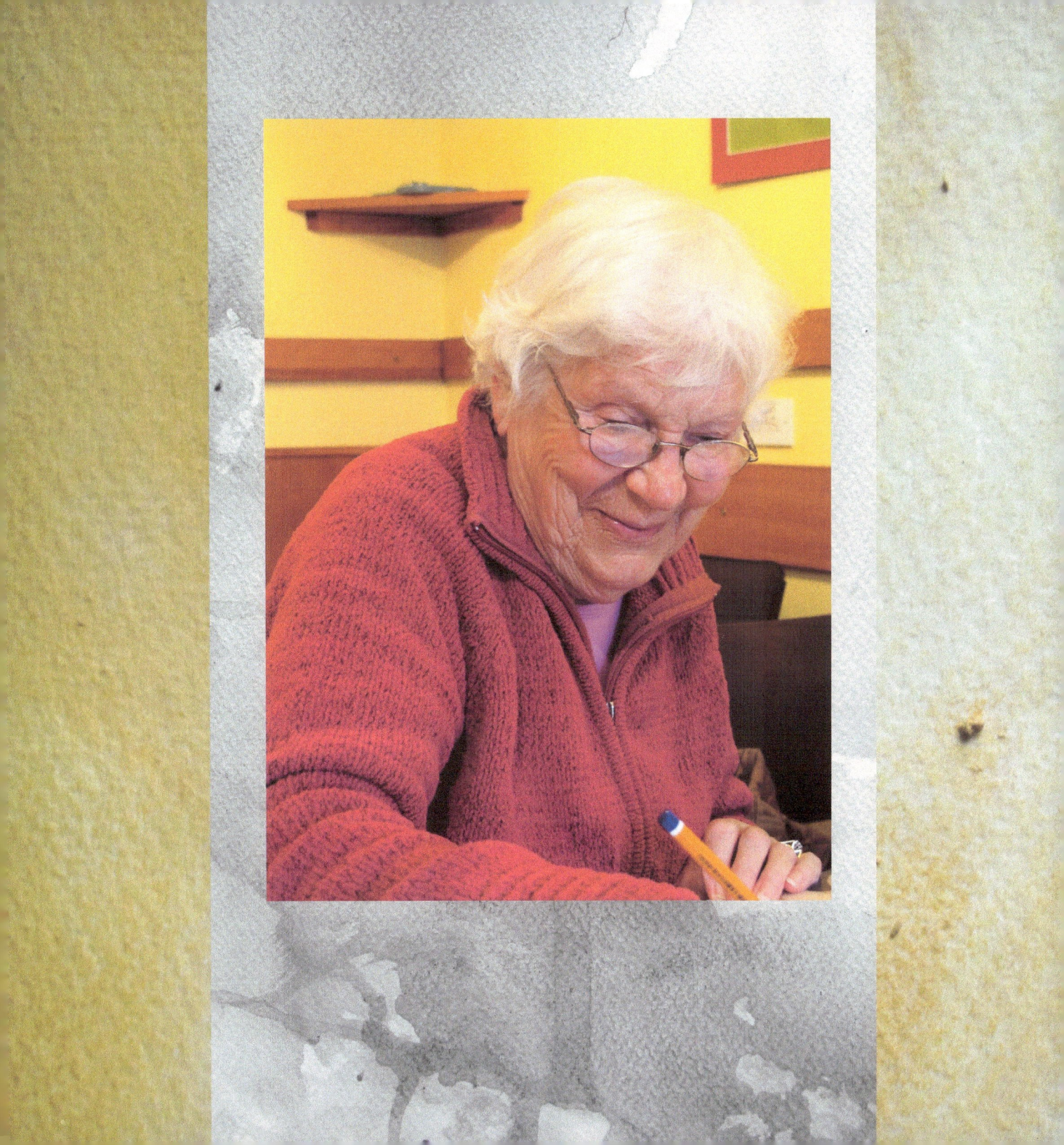

I was born in 1925 in Kilkenny. There was eight of us, four boys and four girls.
I grew up in the country, in the 1930s and 40s, during the war.
My first recollection, my first memories, are of my mother sitting in the kitchen,
in the wintertime by the fire, and she was knitting. She had an extra needle, because
she was doing a cable. I used to watch over her shoulder and she'd be using the extra
needle to put the stitches on, and she was twisting it, and I was intrigued.
So from there I started to knit. I didn't have to, I wanted to. I started on socks, and
then jumpers, and then I started designing cardigans with different panels.
I was always a bit creative. I loved to knit, that was my pastime really.
That and playing tennis.
It didn't only come from my mother, the designing. My father and mother were both
farmers, although neither of them got the family farm. But my father's garden, the
beds and the pathways, the layout of it—it was spectacular.

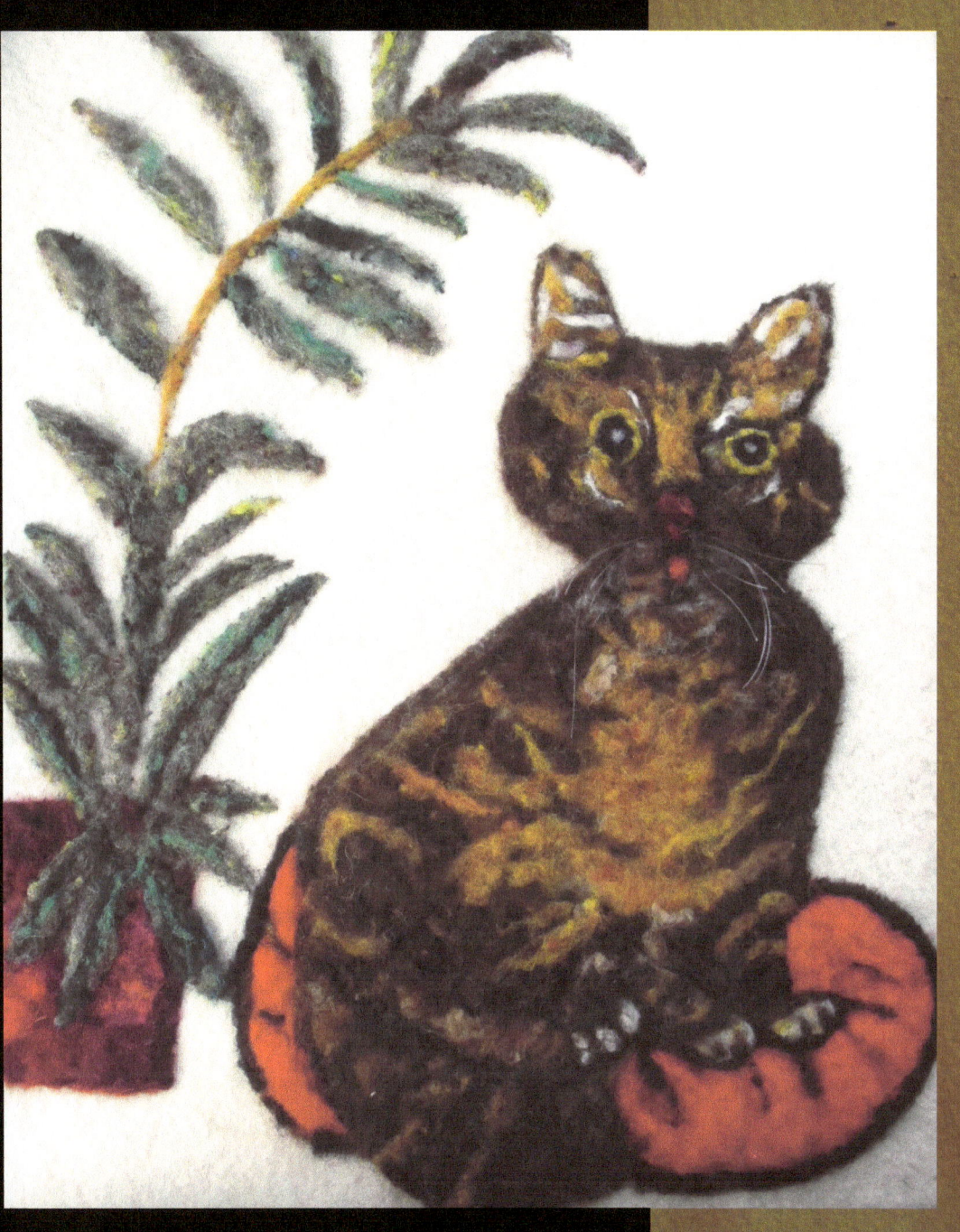

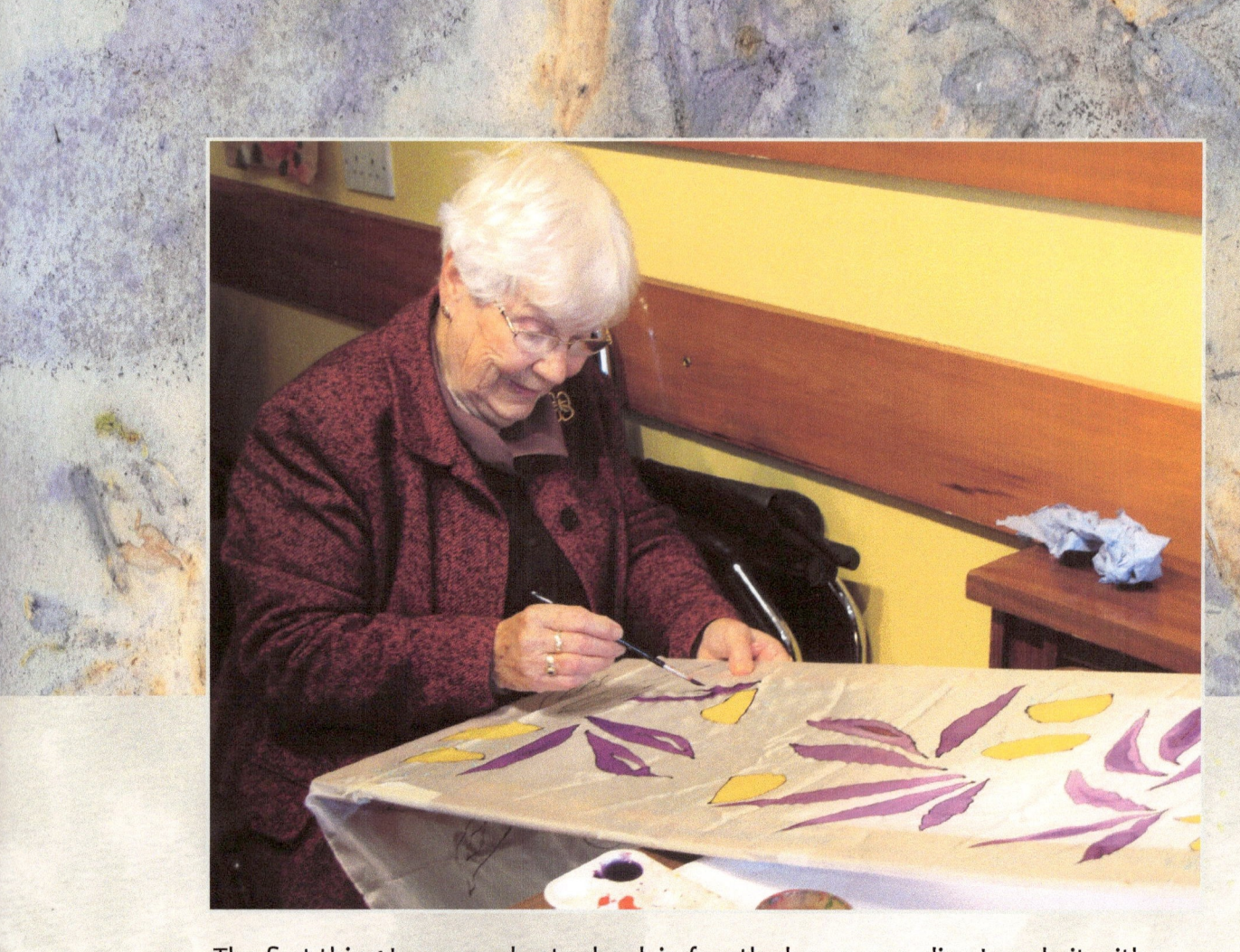

The first thing I ever made at school, in fourth class, was a slip. I made it with crepe de chine or something, silky stuff, and it was pink, no sleeves of course. We hand-stitched it, and I learned to do a run and fell seam.

I went to secondary, and then I did private tuition, ten miles every day on the bike to study commerce. I loved geometry at school, especially Pythagoras's theorem.

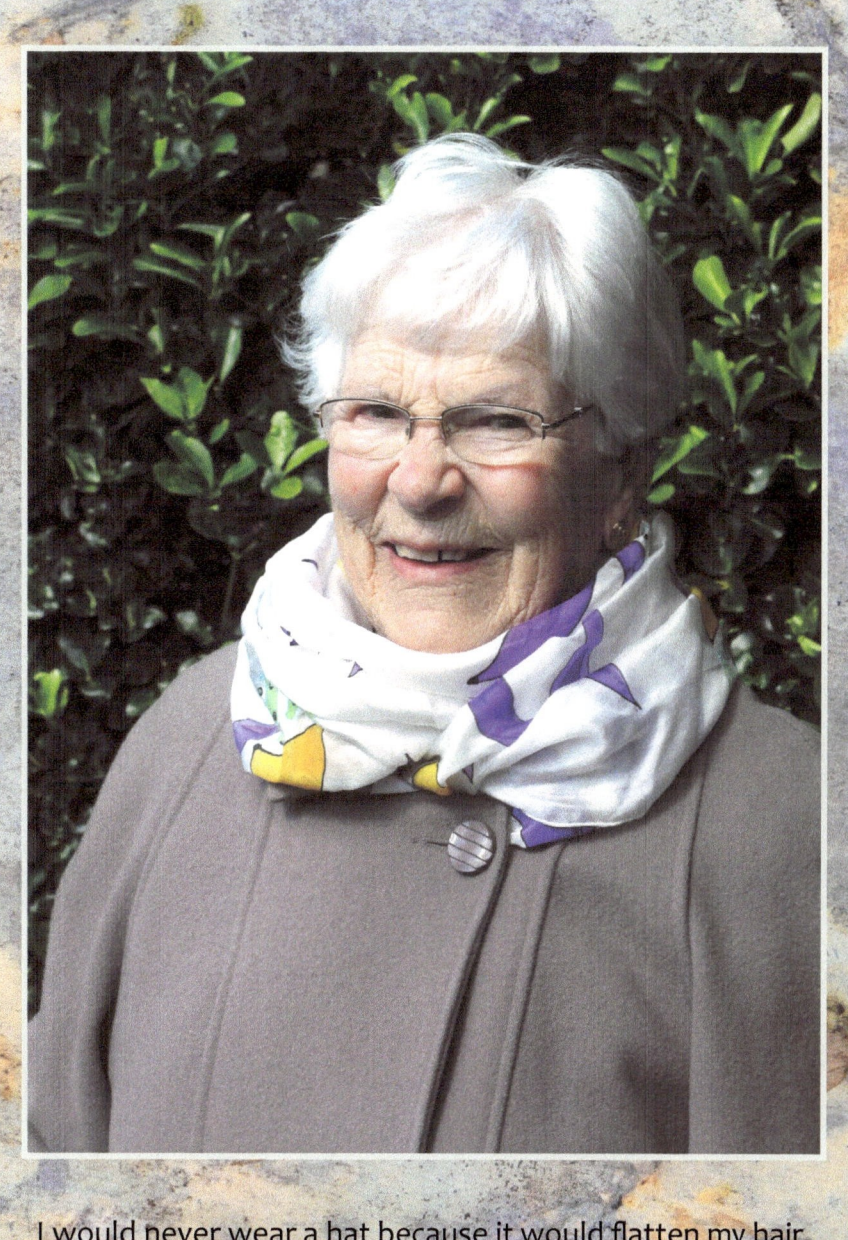

I would never wear a hat because it would flatten my hair.
My mother used to say, "Anna, you're a slave to fashion."
My mother was right you know.

Later I was working in Kilkenny in the office of an insurance company, and at night, in the winter, we'd go to the technical college. It would be something to do, and it was there I must have first made a skirt, a dirndl skirt. You'd buy the material and make a band, measure yourself around the waist, stich along the top, and then you'd pull the threads to make a gathering and stitch it into your band. I thought they were lovely and anyway, that was the skirt you made in those days.

When you were going away on your honeymoon you had to get out of your bridal stuff and change into a going away suit. So I did this in Kilkenny when I got married, and put on a hat and everything. And then when we were out the road my husband Paddy stopped the car and I got into a field and I took all the posh stuff off and I put on a dirndl skirt.

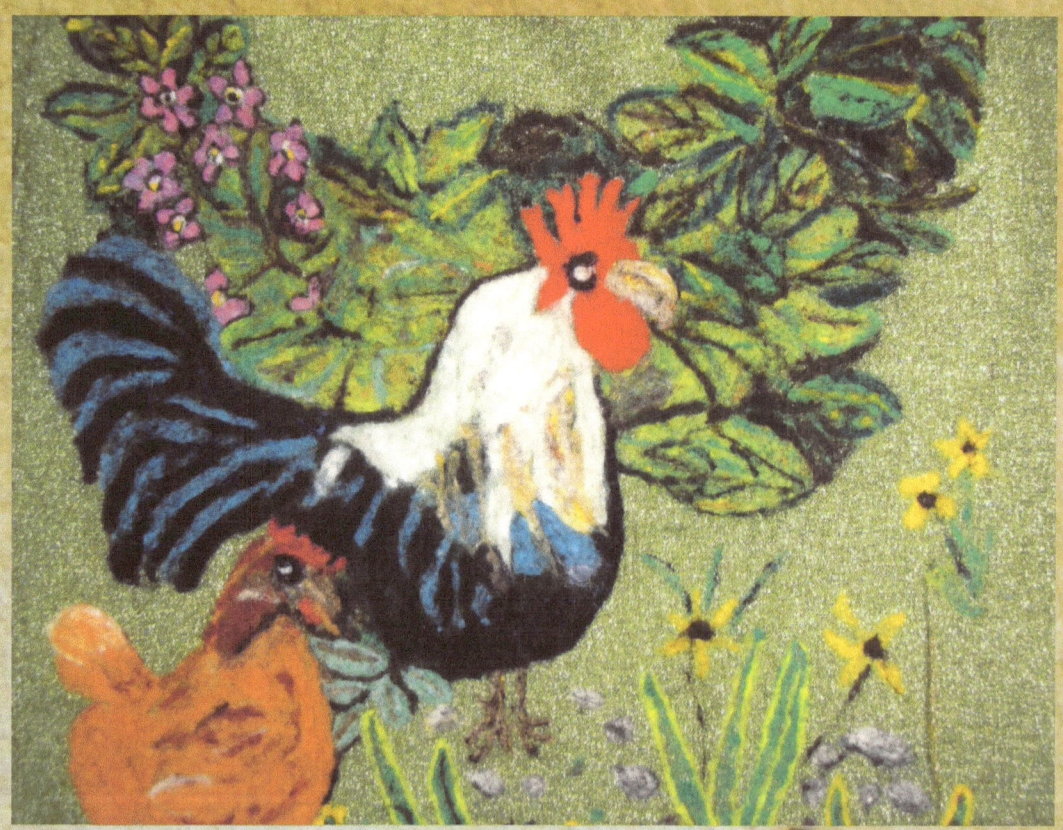

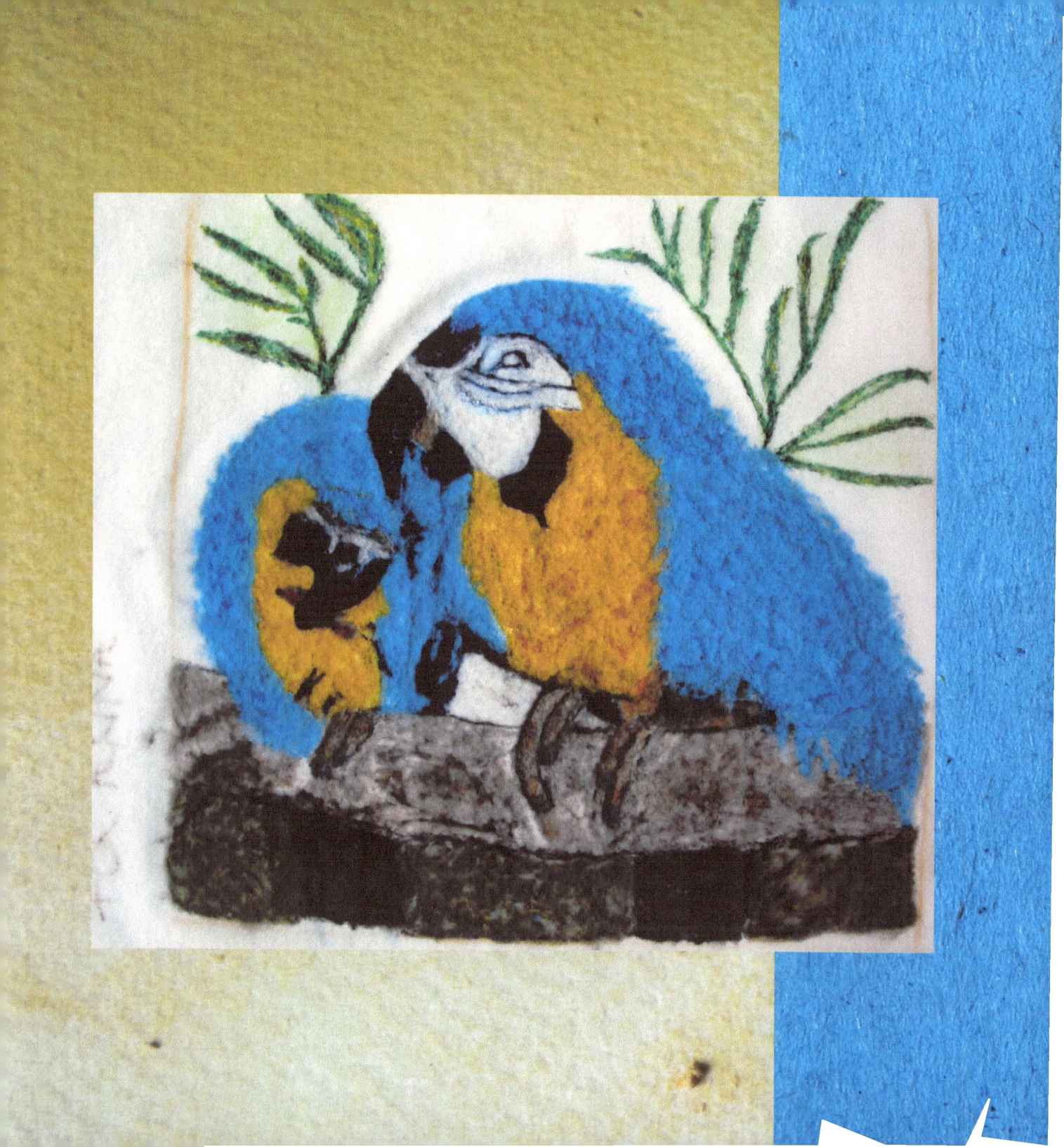

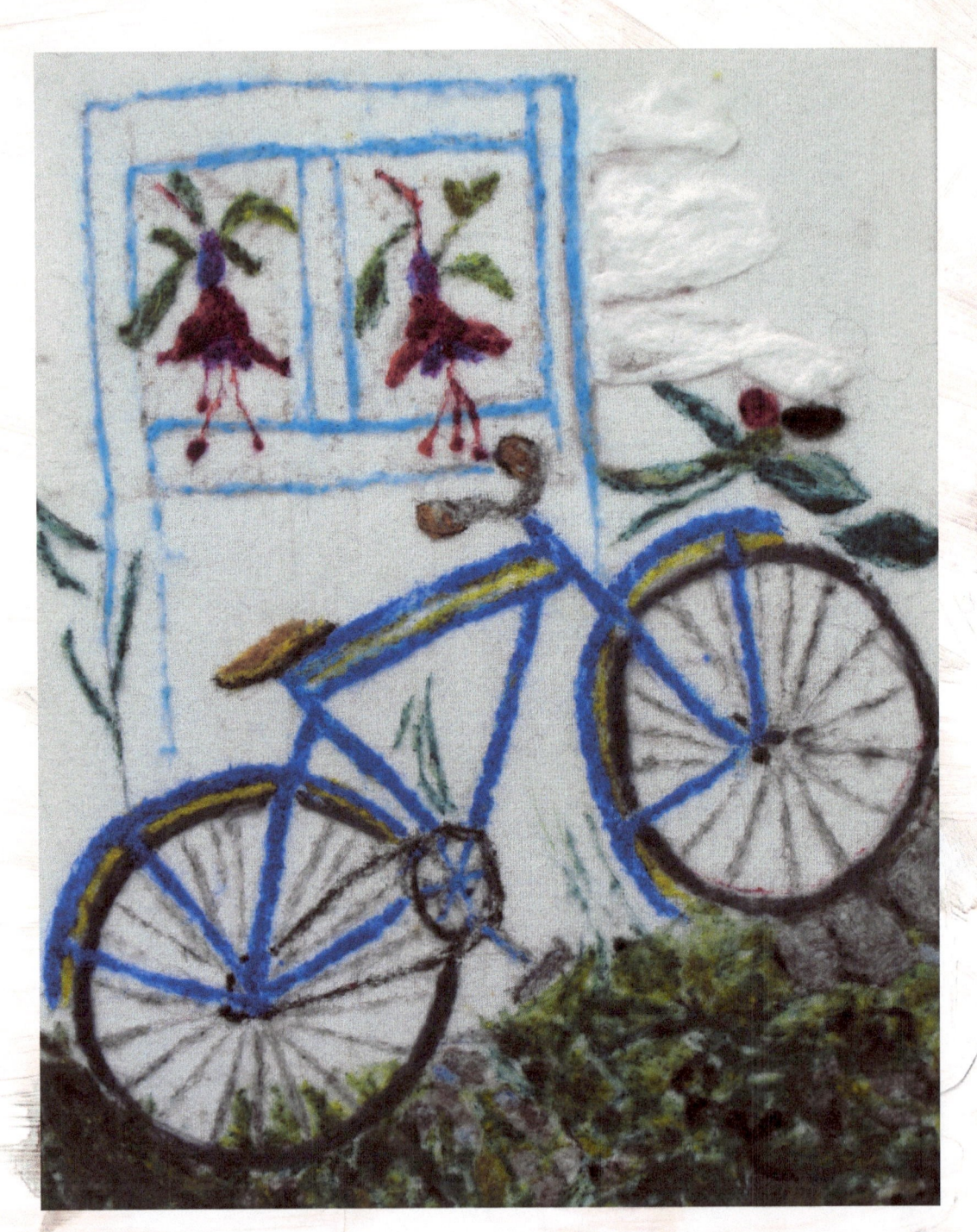

I moved to Dublin in September of 1951.

I went to work in the office of a builders providers, and that's where I met Paddy. In January of 1952, he asked me out. He told me after, that he saw me straight away.

I remember writing to my mother, and saying I'm going out with this fella, his name is Paddy O'Kelly, but I have no notion of becoming Mrs O'Kelly.

I don't know how I said that to her.

He was married to motorbikes. He had three motorbikes at the time, so he had no time for girls, and he was in a motorbike club. They all blamed me then, because when he decided he'd get serious with me, and we were going to get married, he said he couldn't afford to keep the bikes, he couldn't be competitive enough, so he gave them all up.

Once Paddy decided on a thing, he didn't do things by halves.

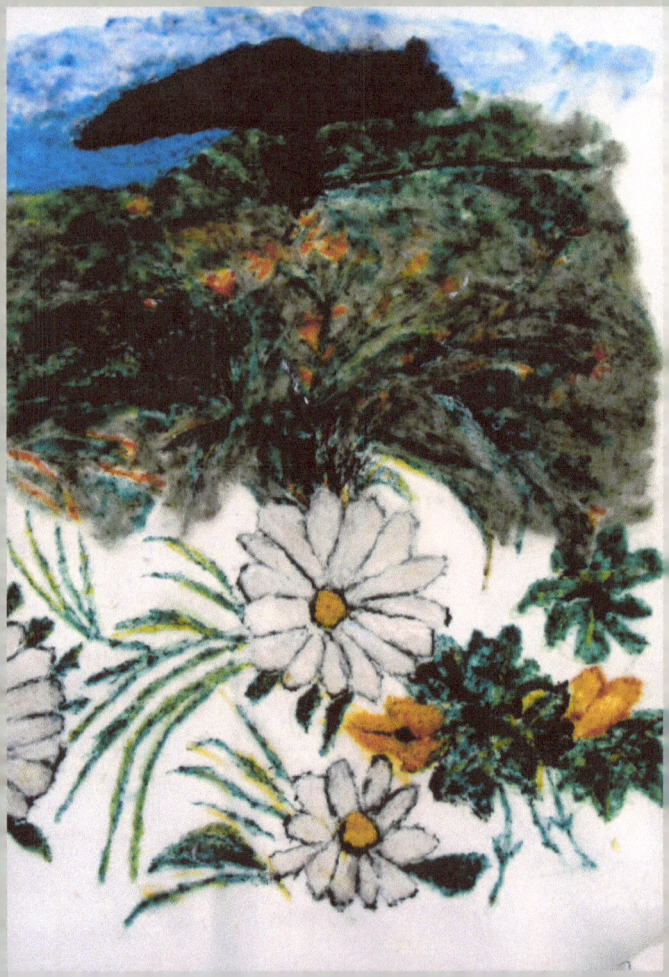

"Kruger" Kavanagh from Dunquin promised my husband Paddy that if he ever got married, he'd give him a week in his hotel. So we came on our honeymoon and he brought me down to Com Dhíneol. As we walked down there were two people on the strand, and Paddy turned to me.

"Anna," he said, "This place is lousy with people." He wanted it all for himself. The weather was marvellous, and I remember we were down in Clogher, and Paddy was nearly crying, when we were going away, because he was leaving Kerry. And I thought I'd never get back to Dublin. Paddy was a Dub, but he was in An Óige, and he used to come cycling, and he fell in love with Kerry.

I was down there today, at Clogher. The waves were crashing, and you couldn't see the sea, it was so full of foam.

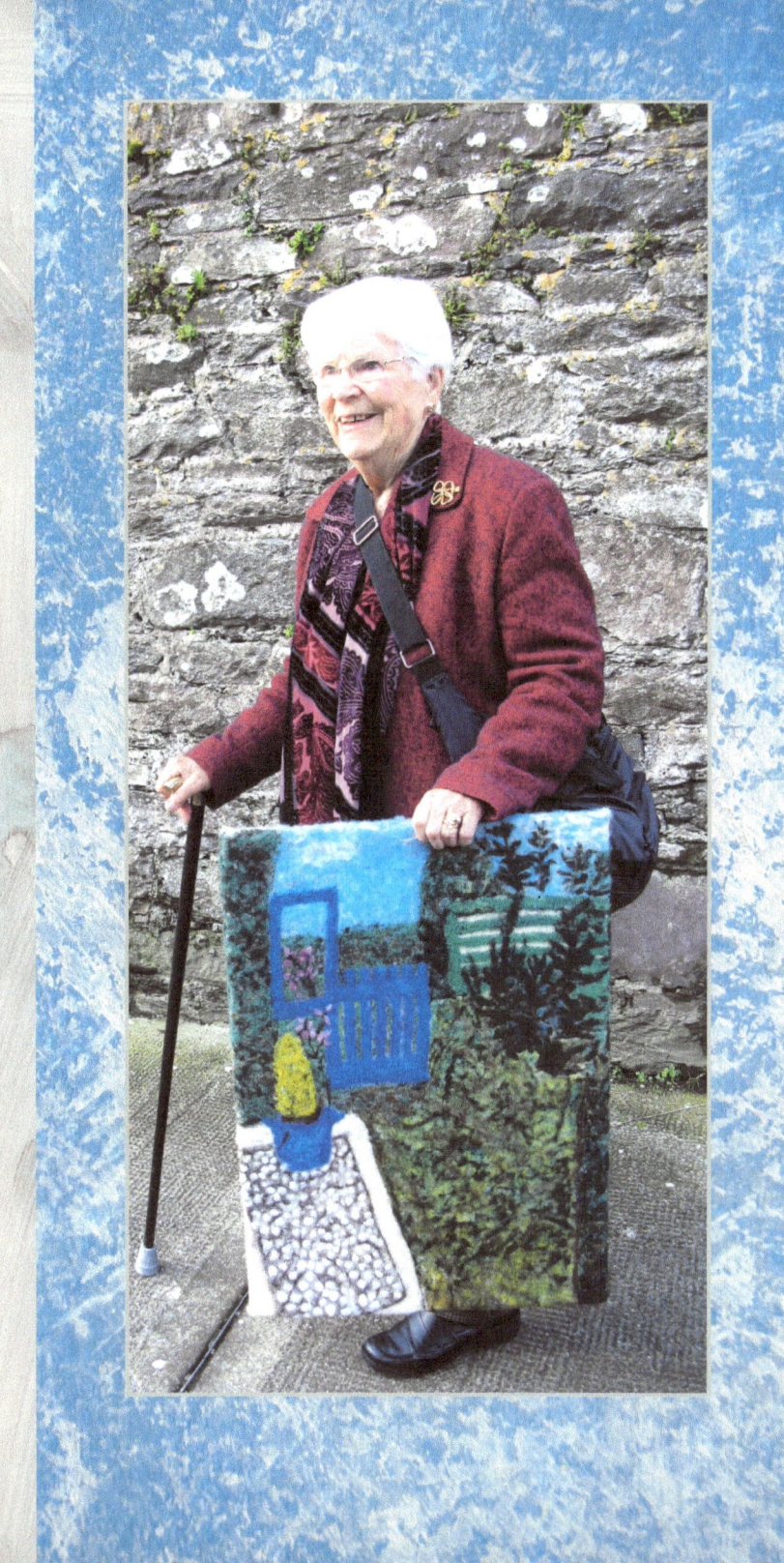

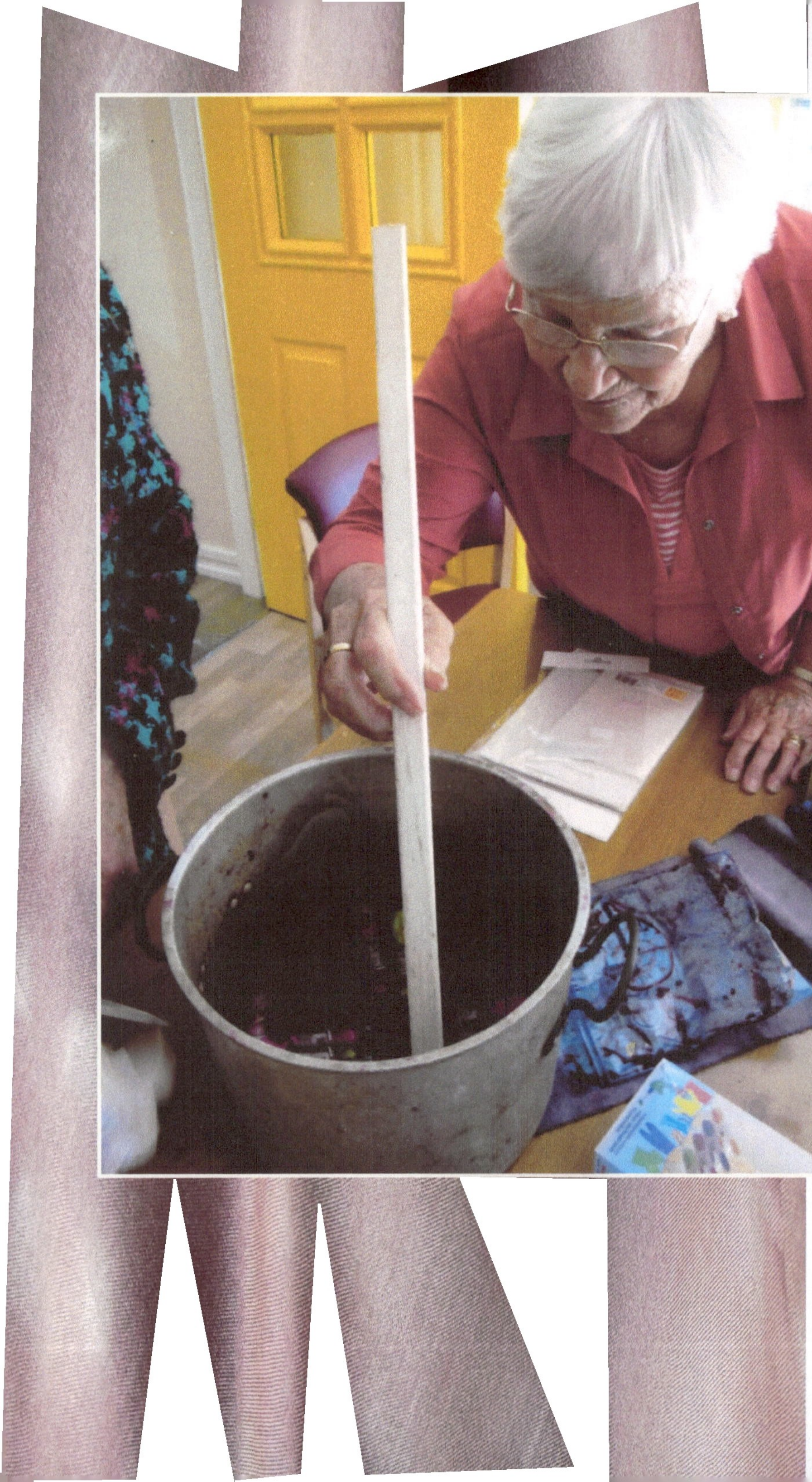

After I was married
I used to go into Dublin.
I'd go into the big stores
and I'd get material
to make dresses,
one for myself
and one for my daughter,
so we were in the same dress—
and I don't think she liked it.
I used to make clothes out of
shirts belonging to my husband.
He was in business, so he'd have
to be dressed properly.
The cuffs and the collar would get
worn and the back of it would be
perfect.
I had a little fella and I made
trousers and a little top for him
out of the shirt.
The sleeves would make the legs
and the rest a little shirt.
It's funny what you remember,
but it's all coming back to me
now.

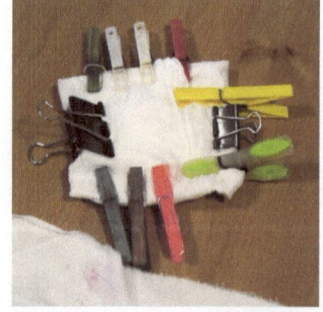

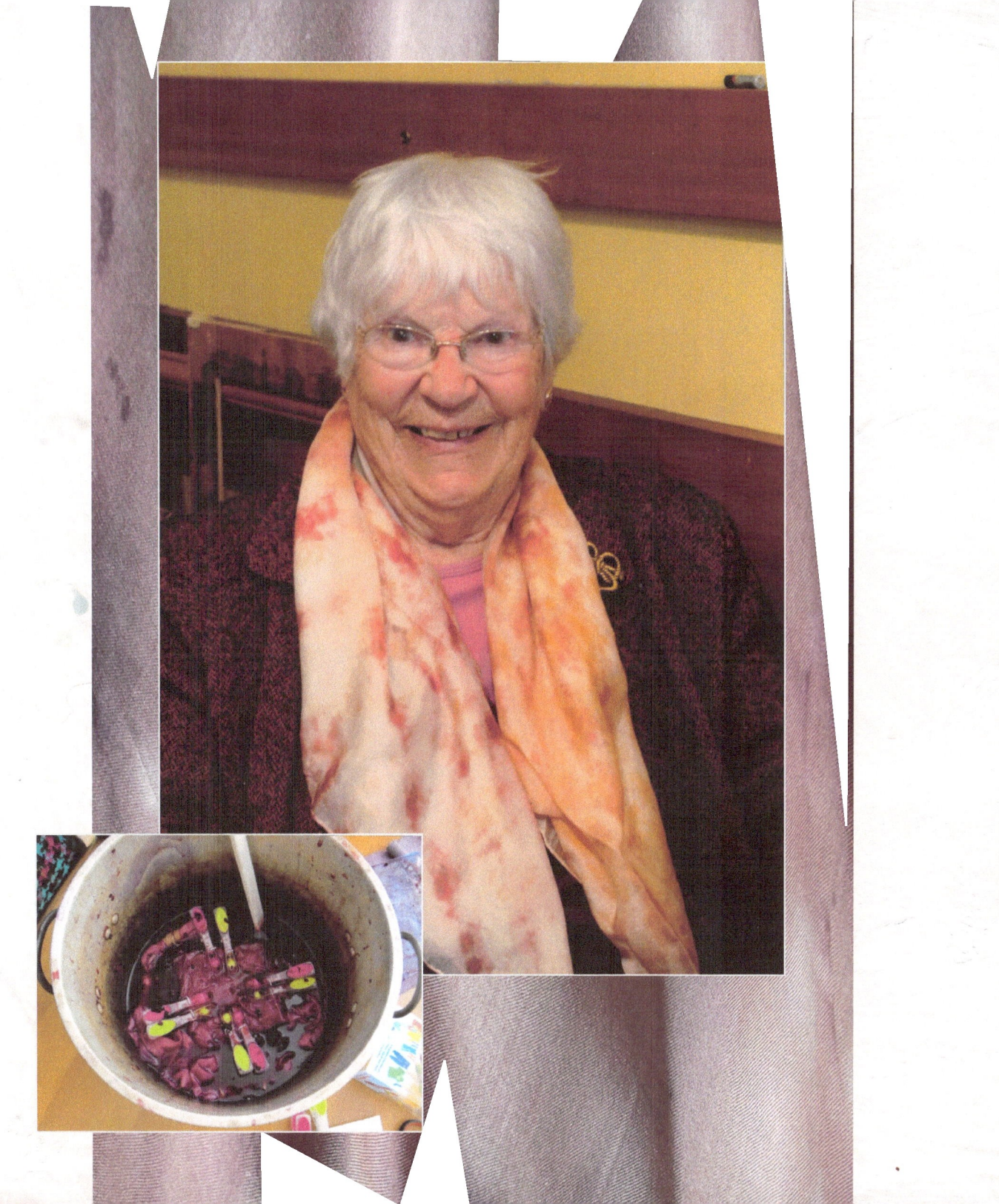

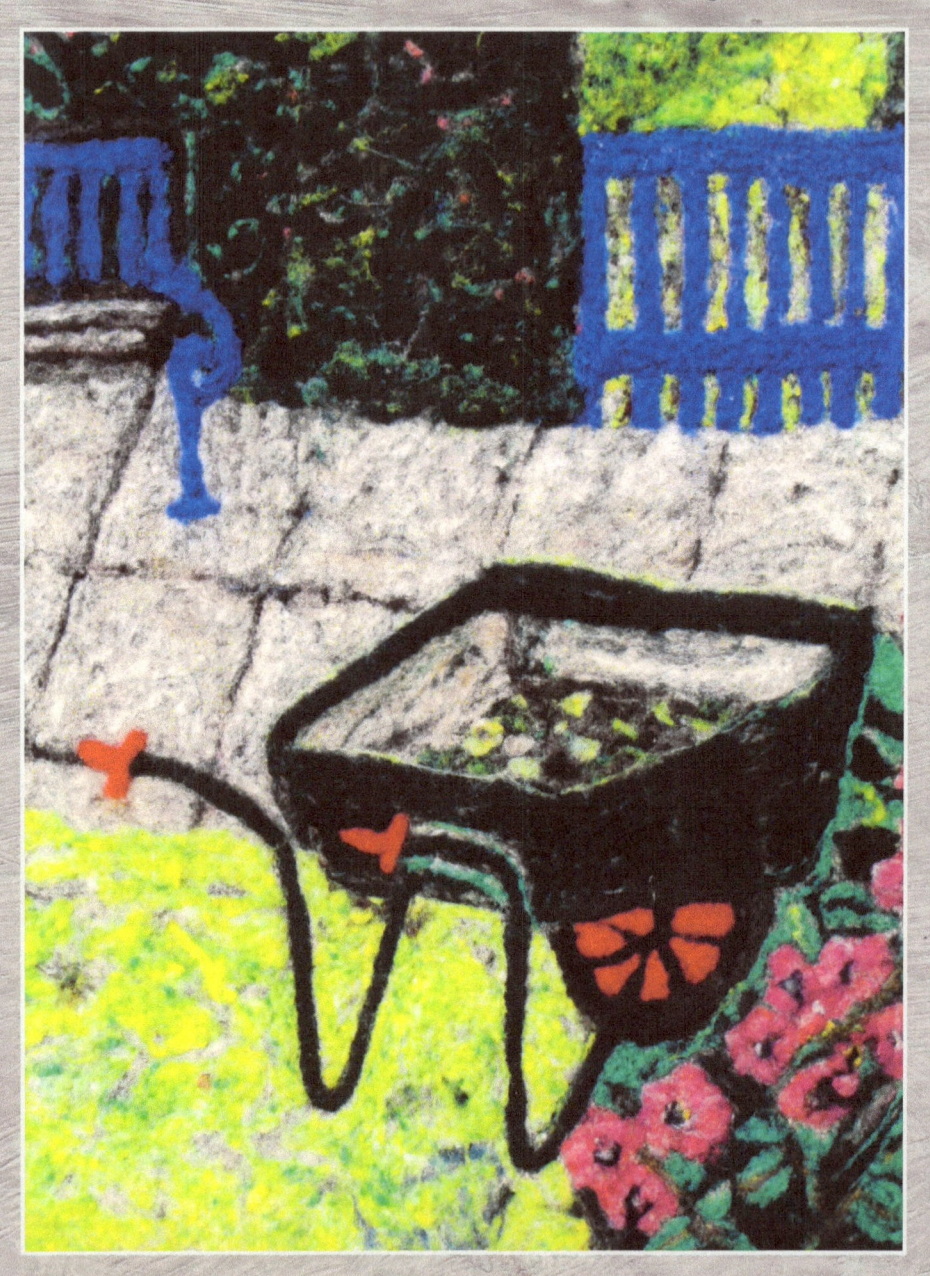

I lived in Dublin for thirty-three years, and I had three children. We used to come to Clogher, camping first and then later a caravan, and eventually we bought the site, and we camped there at first.

The house went up in 1977 I think, and we came here to live in 1984. Paddy planned the house and I planned the garden. And here I am. Thirty years I've been living here now.

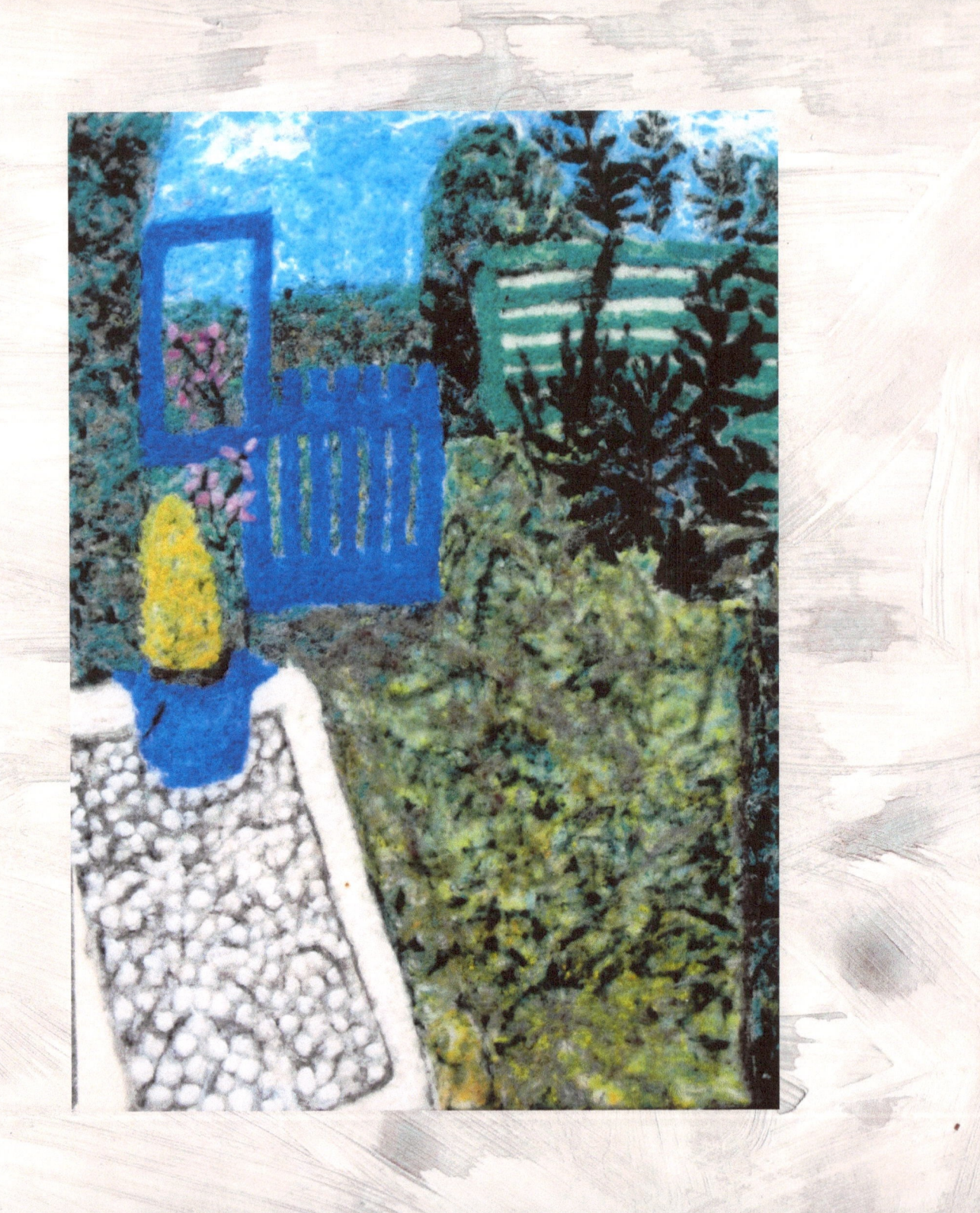

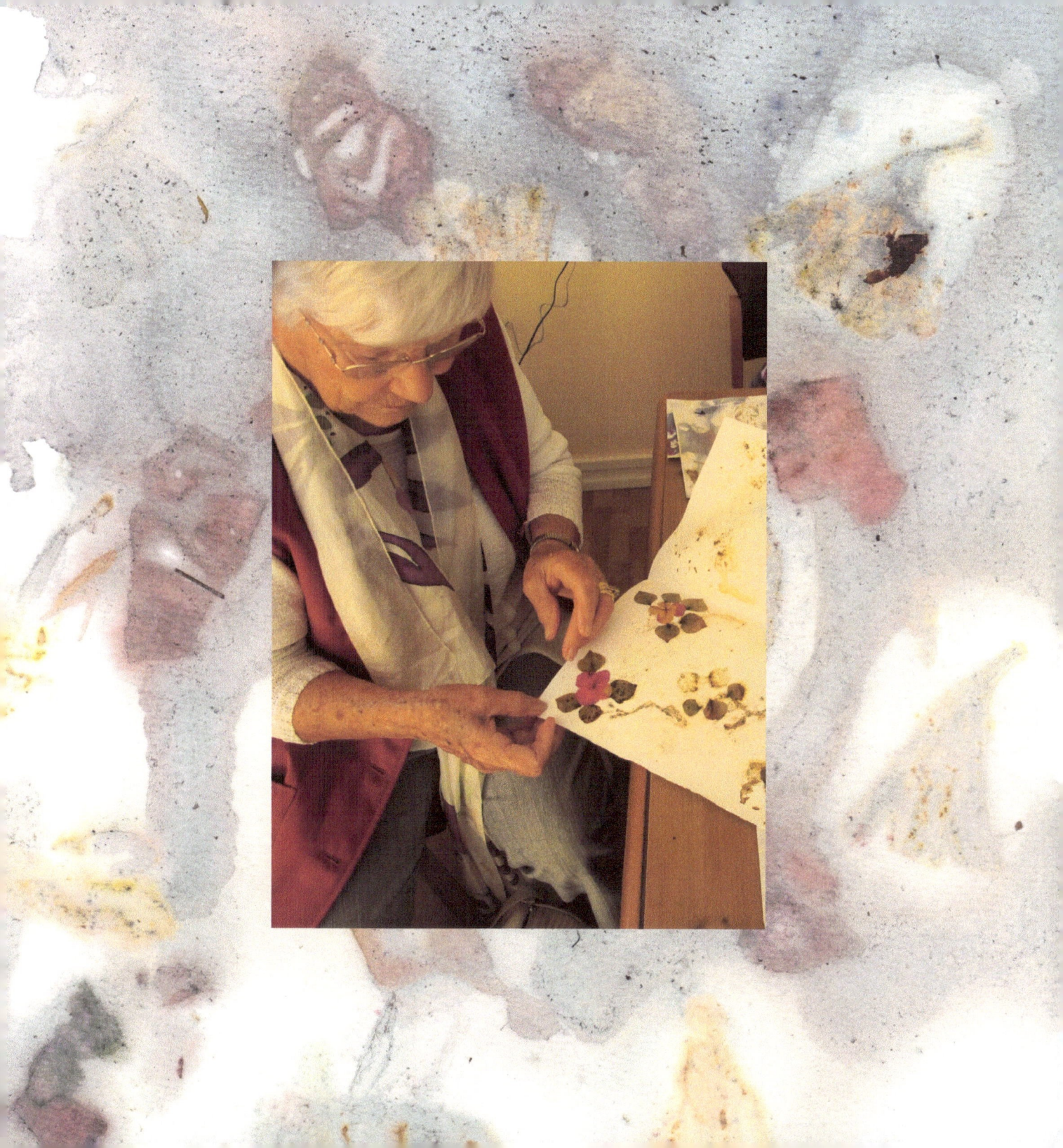

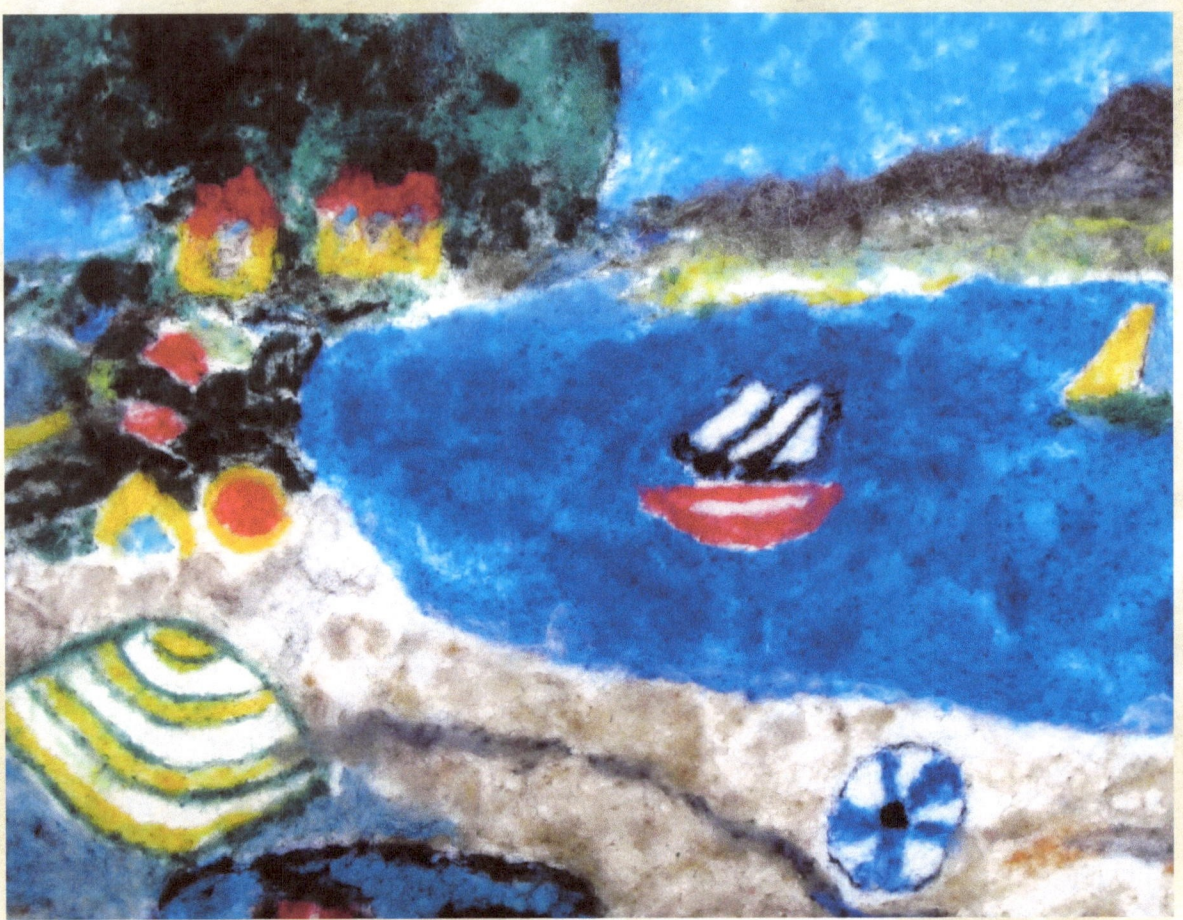

I always thought the women from the rest of Europe, from the continent, were more interested in fashion and design and more glamorous than Irish women. Then I went on holiday to France thirty-five years ago, in the centre of France and different places around. The women there were just the same as the women here.

I was in Spain as well, a long time ago, when they were just starting to build big hotels on the coast, because they were turning it into a tourist spot. The hotel was by the sea and the weather was beautiful, but at the back there were little cottages, where the fishermen and their wives lived, and you may as well have been in Kerry.

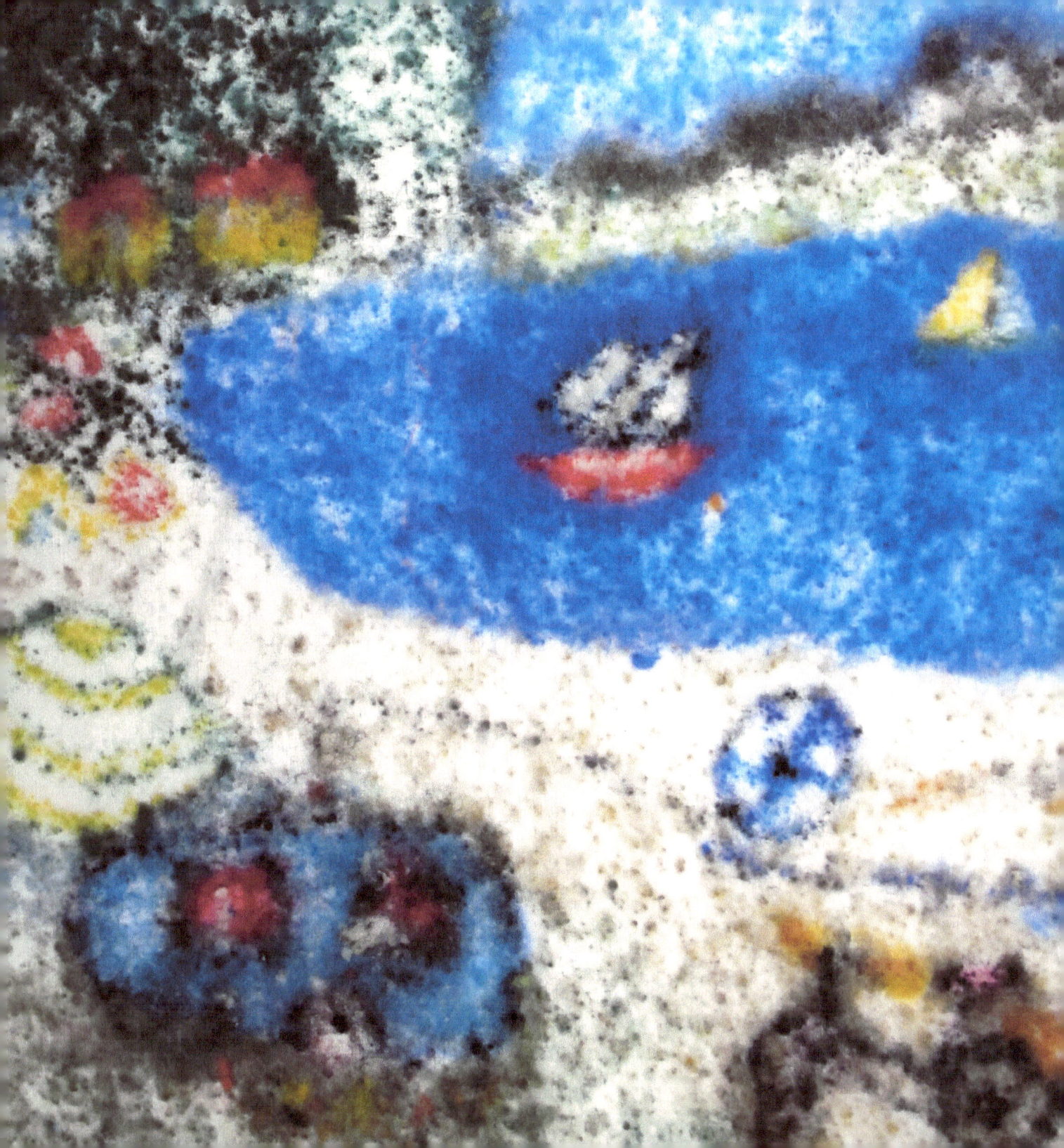

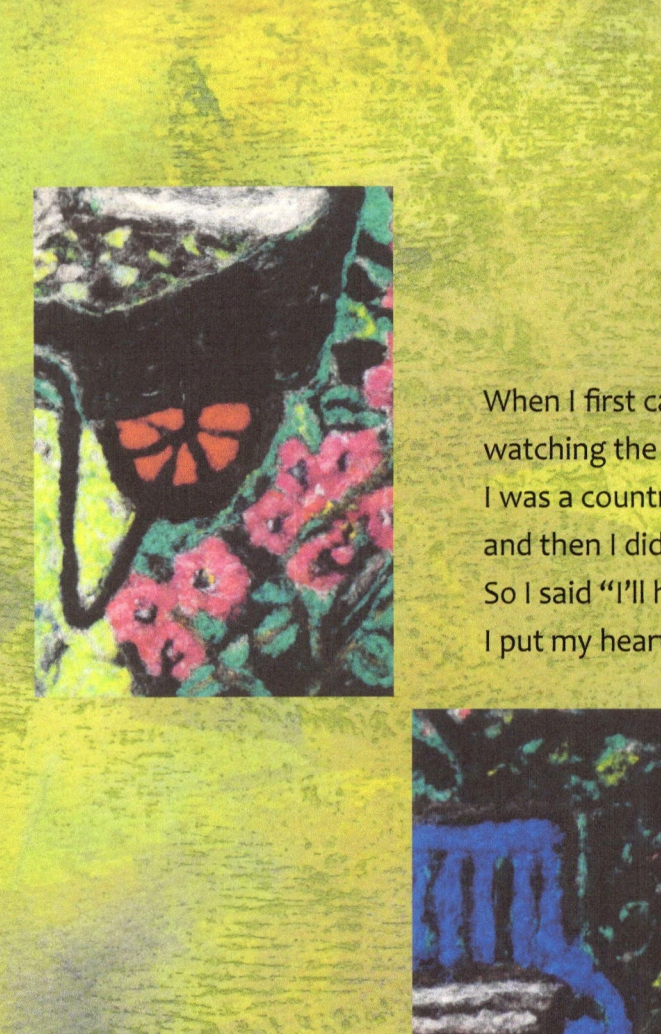

When I first came to live in Kerry, I wasn't good for
watching the beauty of the place.
I was a country girl who got the taste of the city
and then I didn't want the country any more.
So I said "I'll have to do something," and I settled here.
I put my heart into it, and now I wouldn't go back.

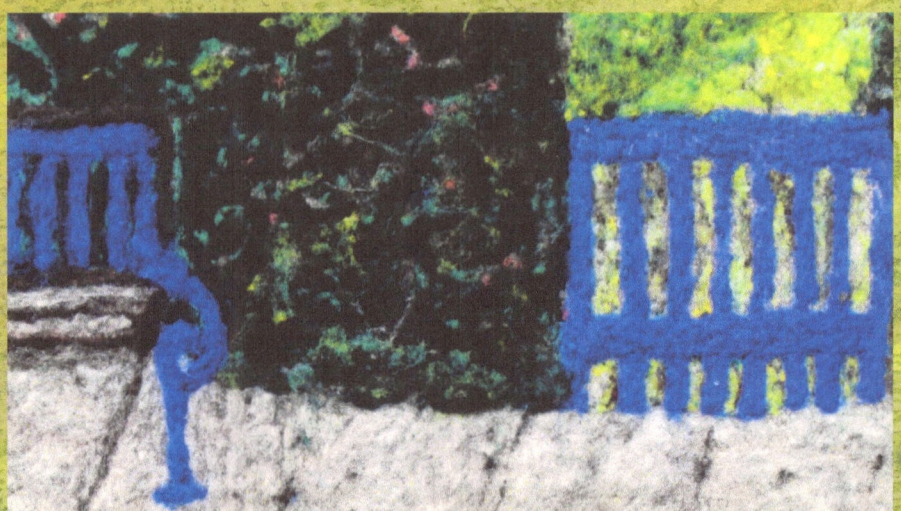

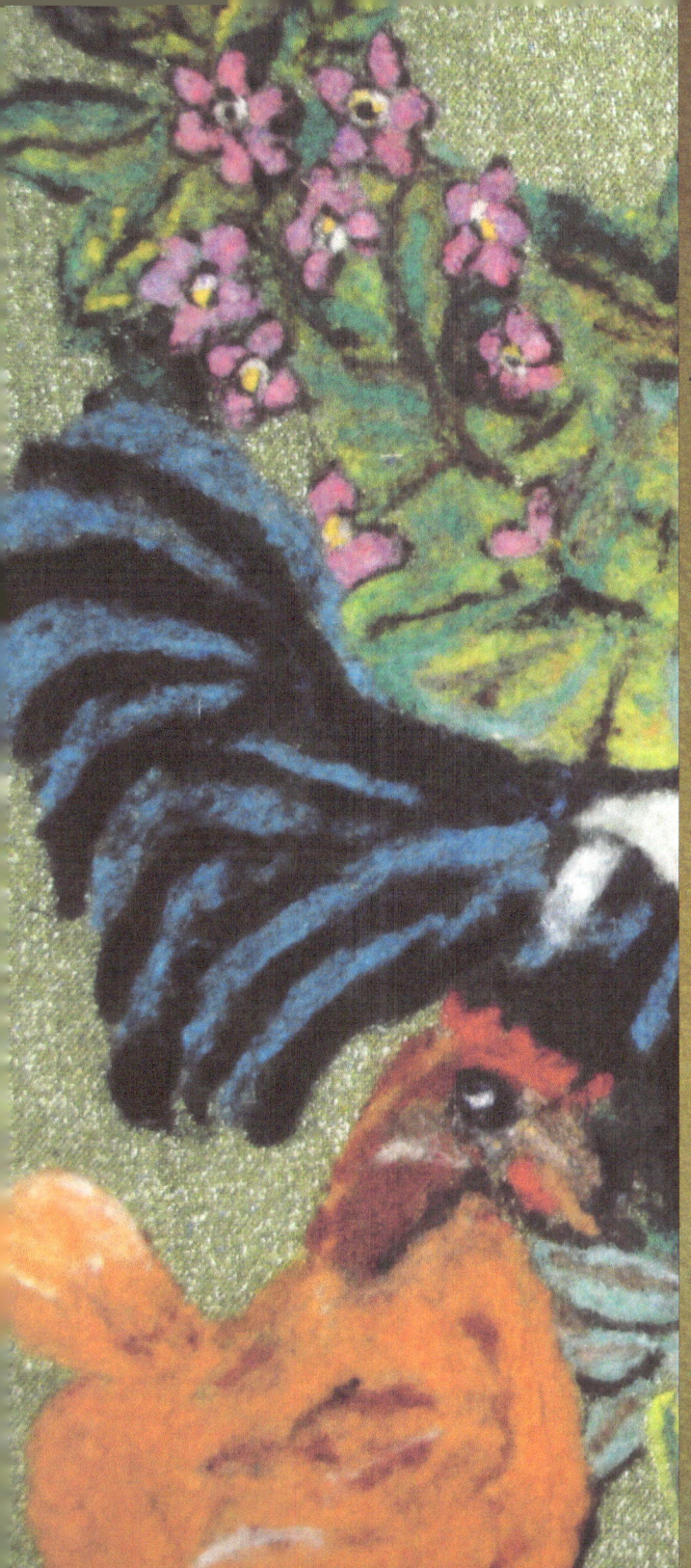

Acknowledgements

We would like to thank everyone who helped in the development of this volume of 'Bealaí Ealaíonta', especially:

Gairdín Mhuire Day Care Centre for older people;

Ealaín na Gaeltachta, for supporting art projects in Gairdín Mhuire;

the Arts Office at Kerry County Council;
Kerry Education and Training Board;
and Anna O'Kelly.

Go raibh míle maith agaibh!

www.ingramcontent.com/pod-product-compliance
Lightning Source LLC
Chambersburg PA
CBHW050913180526
45159CB00007B/2895